Creative Beads
from Paper & Fabric

Create Your Own Crafts & Embellish Ready-
Made Items • No-Sew Fun for All Ages

C&T PUBLISHING

Ann Kristen Krier

Creative beads from paper & fabric
Ann Kristen Krier
Text © 2005, Ann Kristen Krier
Artwork © 2005 C&T Publishing, Inc.
Publisher: Amy Marson
Editorial Director: Gailen Runge
Acquisitions Editor: Jan Grigsby
Editor: Jan Bode Smiley
Proofreader: Wordfirm Inc.
Cover Designer: Kristen Yenche
Design Director/Book Designer: Kristen Yenche
Production Assistant: Matt Allen
Photography: Diane Pedersen and Luke Mulks
Published by C&T Publishing, Inc., P.O. Box 1456, Lafayette, California, 94549

All rights reserved. No part of this work covered by the copyright hereon may be used in any form or reproduced by any means—graphic, electronic, or mechanical, including photocopying, recording, taping, or information storage and retrieval systems—without written permission of the publisher. The copyrights on individual artworks are retained by the artists as noted in <<book title>>.

Attention Teachers: C&T Publishing, Inc. encourages you to use this book as a text for teaching. Contact us at 800-284-1114 or www.ctpub.com for more information about the C&T Teachers Program.

We take great care to ensure that the information included in our books is accurate and presented in good faith, but no warranty is provided nor results guaranteed. Having no control over the choices of materials or procedures used, neither the author nor C&T Publishing, Inc., shall have any liability to any person or entity with respect to any loss or damage caused directly or indirectly by the information contained in this book. For your convenience, we post an up-to-date listing of corrections on our website (www.ctpub.com). If a correction is not already noted, please contact our customer service department at ctinfo@ctpub.com or at P.O. Box 1456, Lafayette, California, 94549.

Trademark (™) and registered trademark (®) names are used throughout this book. Rather than use the symbols with every occurrence of a trademark or registered trademark name, we are using the names only in the editorial fashion and to the benefit of the owner, with no intention of infringement.

Library of Congress Cataloging-in-Publication Data
Krier, Ann,
Creative beads from paper & fabric : create your own crafts & embellish ready made items, no-sew fun for all ages / [text, Ann K. Krier].
p. cm.
Includes index.
ISBN 1-57120-314-1 (paper trade)
1. Beads—Design and construction. 2. Paper work. 3. Textile fabrics.
I. Title.
TT860.K75 2005
745.58'2—dc22
2005003937

Printed in Singapore

10 9 8 7 6 5 4 3 2 1

DEDICATION

For those who create beauty in my world:

Jim, Mike, Brett, and Maggie Sue

ACKNOWLEDGMENTS

To the staff of If It's Paper!, and the Enchanted Cottage Winston-Salem, NC, for sharing their knowledge of paper, inks, and stamping and for their encouragement.

To the staff of C&T Publishing for working with a new author.

To my aunts Ethel and Frances Dann, and Boni Overslaugh who always took the time to play sewing or teach us a new craft.

To my friends Terry Ann Linden, Debra, Fran, and Ruth, for pats on the back. To my mother, who let me use her new Singer sewing machine to make clothes. Thanks for that and all the other gifts you have given me.

To my children, Brett and Maggie Sue, for their companionship and compliments during "mommy's art projects."

Most importantly, to my beloved husband, Jim, who has always supported my ideas—even the bad ones; who is quick to encourage me when I am unsure; who reminds us all to take time to play; who works hard so that I can buy more fabric and paper. Without his support, none of this would be possible.

Thank you all.

Contents

INTRODUCTION

Creative Beads from Paper and Fabric presents a wonderful opportunity to expand your creativity. The materials and techniques used are readily available from retail stores, the recycling bin, and craft supplies you already own. You will quickly become immersed in the relative ease of the process and projects included in this book. Together, we'll follow a natural progression, from selecting materials for creating the beads to making them into miniature works of art. Once you have mastered the basics of construction, you can explore several techniques to expand your newfound talents. Whether you are five, fifty, or one hundred and five, you can enjoy this easy form of paper and fiber art.

Every process presented in this book has been thoroughly researched, practiced, and refined. The mess, the expense of trial and error, and the guesswork have already been completed for you. The results of my experiences are shared with you throughout this book.

You will quickly discover that there is no exact science to making paper and fabric beads, which is part of their beauty. Although I offer tips and tricks to help you master your bead techniques, you will most likely develop your own set of tricks. I hope you enjoy the process and the discoveries along the way.

HISTORY OF BEAD MAKING

Creativity and adornment have historically been an important part of daily life. Beads have been a staple in fashion and decoration since their origin some 40,000 years ago. Beads span history by creating a statement about the creator, the wearer, and the culture in which they were made.

By looking at beads, we can learn about the culture and the bead maker. Italian bead artisans are famous for their millefiori glass beads, which showcase exquisite glass-blowing talent and a fine understanding of color. Bead makers on the island of Bali are highly regarded for their silver filigree work, which displays elaborate metallurgic techniques and a fondness for ornate design. Third world countries in Africa use readily available natural materials to create rustic earth-tone beads, honoring their ancestral tradition of using beads for trade and commerce. All of these beads have a story to tell about the culture and geographical makeup of the country where they were created.

These small pieces of art are a vital contribution to a society's culture. You can use the techniques in *Creative Beads from Paper and Fabric* to expand on the enduring tradition of beads by creating original art to leave your own creative mark on the world.

Bead art also offers solace and community. Some cultures assign healing powers to certain beads. Beads can help you expand your creativity or sustain you in your comfort zone, while you forge new friendships with like-minded "beaders."

While many of the ideas included in this book were created on a whim, it is in celebration of the creative spirit and in sharing the joys of working with both fibers (paper and fabric) and beads that I offer *Creative Beads from Paper and Fabric;* a collection of techniques and projects to inspire creativity.

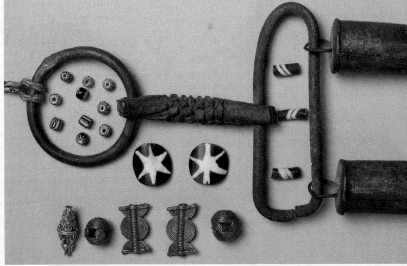

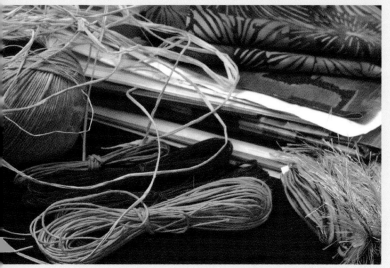

What is FIBER ART?

In the arts and crafts world, fibers are used for surface interest. Woven into a basket, handloomed into a rug, incorporated into a wallhanging, integrated into a collage, hand embroidered, or sewn into a quilt—fiber is a very versatile medium. Whatever type of artwork you do, you can expand your creativity by combining it with fiber.

Chapter 1

Fiber art encompasses any creative pursuit that incorporates fiber. In its simplest form, a fiber is any long slender thread or filament. Natural fibers include cotton, flax, wood, grass, or animal wool. Synthetic fibers include Tencel and nylon. Fibers can be used exclusively in your artwork, added as embellishments, or combined with other mediums for an entirely new look. Readily available fibers include yarn, textiles, and paper.

Fiber arts benefit from texture, tactile appeal, and three-dimensional opportunities; after all, who can resist reaching out to touch soft fabrics, interesting yarns, or paper sculptures. Including fiber in your work adds to the viewer's enjoyment.

WHAT ARE FIBER ART BEADS?

Fiber art beads are simply beads made from fibers, which are used to create a soft, textured bead. When using fabric as the fiber, the fabric creates the bead. Likewise, you can manipulate yarns to form the bead. You can create beads by combining fibers with a machine, with heat, or with adhesive. You can then embellish any of these basic beads with yarns, other fibers, beads, or even wire.

If you've never worked with traditional fiber before, don't despair. The techniques for creating the beads are very easy. You might even want to adapt the processes to use with other materials that can be folded, rolled, and joined with thread or glue. Throughout the book, instruction and inspiration will be shown in a variety of materials.

Selecting MATERIALS

As with any new process, following basic guidelines will help ensure a satisfactory outcome. I offer tips along the way to help your process go smoothly. Some of this information may seem obvious, but it will help provide you with a successful experience making Creative Beads from Paper and Fabric.

Chapter 2

BEAD BODY MATERIALS
Fabric Types

If you are already a fabric junkie, you will enjoy making beads from your stash and scraps. If you are new to the fabric world, welcome! But be forewarned, collecting fabric can be extremely addictive.

A variety of fabric

There seems to be no end to the variety of fabrics on the market today, and many of them are perfect for the techniques shared in this book. You won't need great quantities of fabric; the smallest bits of favorite fabrics can be used to their full potential. Don't limit yourself to shopping only at the fabric store; think about recycling threadbare clothing, cutting up old fabric napkins, or featuring cherished but damaged vintage linens.

If you are purchasing new fabric, almost any lightweight material will do, including cotton, cotton blend, polyester, silk, rayon, lightweight wool, or synthetic fiber. The most important thing is for the fabric to be flexible. In other words, the fabric must be capable of being cut, then folded, twisted, or shaped.

tip

When choosing fabric for your beads, avoid heavy-weight fabrics such as denim, canvas, and upholstery materials, since they are typically not flexible enough to make satisfactory beads.

Also, when selecting materials, keep in mind that nonpermeable fabric will require a different adhesive, or perhaps wire, to hold the bead together. Permeable fabrics, on the other hand, will absorb traditional adhesives, which usually makes them easier to use.

There is one notable exception to the above comments: leather and suede make fabulous beads. The tactile sense of these materials far outweighs the difficulty you might have when rolling them. Use special leather adhesives and a slightly larger form, perhaps a size 5 or 7 knitting needle. You can purchase small scraps of leather at craft stores; you can also use discarded samples from an interior design firm. Remember, you don't need much to make a terrific bead.

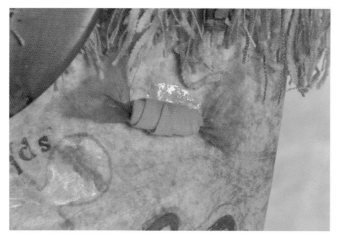

Suede leather bead

tip

Remember, this information is a guideline only: you can vary your results with fabric type, color, or texture—or all three!

Fabric Textures

Texture is one attribute of fiber that can be used to your advantage when making creative beads. You might choose textured felt, silk dupioni, nubby linen, or tropical-weight wools. But keep in mind that the bulkier the fabric, the more difficult it can be to manipulate. By incorporating texture, your beads will have depth and varied surface interests which is an important aspect of fiber art.

Paper Types

Perhaps you remember making paper beads when you were in kindergarten. During the Victorian Era, women of all ages made paper beads. Because blank paper was not in abundance, they made beads from old catalogs, newspapers, and meat wrappers and then strung these beads onto long threads and hung them in doorways as curtains. Making good use of potential waste paper, these ladies represented the ultimate in recycling!

Like fabric, paper is available in an incredible variety of weights, colors, and textures. If you already have a collection of beautiful papers, you probably have hundreds of design ideas going through your mind at this very moment. If you are new to the paper art world, consider purchasing a "scrap pack" from the craft store. These smaller sizes are perfect for making beads and give you a variety of paper with a minimal investment. Although many of us are drawn to handmade paper for its texture, rest assured that you can have marvelous results by using newspaper, magazine pages, wrapping paper, candy and gum wrappers, juice pouches, fancy paper napkins, or old catalogs just as easily as Victorian women did.

Paper Weights

Papers, like fabrics, come in different weights; heavier weight papers require more adhesive and will result in a fatter bead. When making beads, paper usually requires longer strips than fabric; the added length of the paper strip adds strength to the finished bead.

Vellum is a smooth, translucent paper that comes in great colors and prints and a variety of themes. Making vellum into beads intensifies the paper's translucent qualities. Stacking different colored vellums together in small quantities to make a bead is a great way to use this medium and to create new colors. See Double-Layered Beads (page 22) for more information. By placing vellums on top of another material, you can subdue intense colors or images.

Vellum layer on notecard

Handmade paper is another fascinating material that yields wonderful beads. Handmade papers are loved for their heft and texture. Make your own handmade paper using the variety of books and kits available (see Resources on page 46), or purchase handmade paper in individual sheets or packs.

Tissue papers and mulberry papers are admired for their ethereal quality. Both are very soft to the touch, but, when glued, they often discolor or allow the colors to run. To minimize this problem, use a glue stick (a dry adhesive) when gluing these papers.

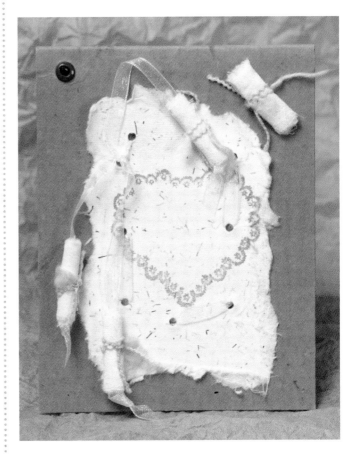

Paper Textures

Papers of different weights have a different hand (feel), or texture, that makes them a great choice for making creative beads. Choose papers for your bead adventures based on their tactile appeal as well as their suitability. Heavier weight papers will require more patience when making the bead and more creative solutions for securing it.

In some aspects, working with paper is easier than working with fabric. In other aspects, however, it is more difficult. Paper rips more easily and is more likely to absorb the adhesive and become damp. Therefore, you might need a bit more patience when working with paper.

Nonwoven Materials

Nonwoven and other nontraditional materials, such as Dupont's Tyvek, are finding their way into the toolboxes of many paper and textile artists. You've probably been using these materials for years in the form of nonwoven interfacings, mailing envelopes, and synthetic felt.

Tyvek, the fiber in Federal Express Paks and priority mail envelopes from the United States Postal Service, is the best of fabric, paper, and fiber—all rolled into one material. Tyvek can be dyed, painted, sanded, stamped, or sewn. When heated, this material forms unique shapes and results in beads with great durability. Tyvek offers one of the easiest ways of achieving an aged effect for your beads. Refer to Heat Shrink Beads (page 31) to find out the many ways of coloring Tyvek using pigment inks.

Beads made from Tyvek or interfacing

Recycle the inside of used Federal Express and U.S. Express or Priority Mail envelopes. You can paint or dye this material to your liking. The printed side will be rolled into your bead, and no one will ever see it!

Interfacing is another versatile material for bead making; you can sew it, embroider it, dye it, or alter it with a heat tool. Experiment with different weights to achieve similar looks with varied textures.

Some synthetic battings also make great beads. When heat is applied, some areas melt, creating a lacey effect. While the results are unpredictable, the surface can be a wonderful canvas to highlight with paints or pigment powders.

To avoid breathing the fumes that result from altering synthetic materials, heat them outdoors.

Nonwoven tissue is another interesting product for making beads. It comes in approximately 25 solid colors and, in most techniques, reacts in a manner similar to paper. Unlike paper, however, the nonwoven tissues are semitransparent, strong when wet, and dense, which means you will use far less material to achieve the same results as with regular tissue. You can also layer nonwoven tissues for an interesting effect.

Check your local specialty paper store or the Internet for nonwoven tissue. It is available in 20″ x 30″ sheets and in marvelously brilliant colors. This nonwoven material, already colored and waterproof, can yield incredibly creative beads.

Don't be afraid of color. It is often the greatest component of your design. *Use it.*

FIBERS

Thread, yarn, ribbon, wire, and embroidery floss are all fibers that you can use to enhance your paper and fabric beads. You can also use them instead of adhesive to hold the bead together. Whether you choose a fiber for fashion or function, some basic knowledge is helpful.

The variety of colors and textures in fibers—whether made from natural or synthetic materials—is unlimited. Use your imagination and enjoy the hunt for interesting fibers. Unravel yarns from old sweaters, recycle leftovers from an embroidery project, select fibers from the pile of scraps under your cutting table, or purchase new fibers at art and craft stores.

The most important attribute to keep in mind when selecting fibers is how you are going to make the bead and what you will use it for. If you know a bead will be exposed to heat during the creation process, don't use a synthetic polymer fiber; it will melt when you heat the bead. However, adding this same fiber *after* the bead has been heated and cooled may yield great results! Choosing a fiber that has no holding power will create problems in wearable art that will be laundered. Making a fiber body bead of loose fibers for use on an everyday purse will probably wear the bead "bald" after a while; however, loose fibers would be fine for a special-occasion bag. Keep the final project in mind when selecting your fibers and you will be assured that your hard work in creating the beads is not wasted.

Fiber Strength

When selecting fibers to use for tying your beads, consider both strength and bulk. The stronger the fiber, the better it will hold. The bulkier the fiber, the more likely it will untie itself on your finished beads. Untying can be overcome with a spot of glue on the final knot; or consider hand sewing the fiber onto the bead. Whatever you choose, pay attention to the fiber, and adapt your techniques as necessary.

Fiber Types

Look at the craft store for interesting "eyelash" yarns and metallic embroidery floss. Consider buying variegated skeins to instantly increase your color selection. Natural raffia and wool are other interesting options for tying your beads.

Adding a touch of glue to the final knot can secure even the slipperiest fiber, while adding sparkle to your finished bead.

FORMS

Forms are the bases that the fiber, fabric, or paper will be wrapped around when making your beads. When selecting a form, think about what shape you want the finished bead to have, as well as the techniques that you will use for making and embellishing the bead.

Typical forms are smooth-surfaced cylinders such as straws or coffee stirrers, fat toothpicks, a wooden skewer, a knitting needle, a screwdriver, nails, or even chopsticks. Be sure you can roll the form with one hand while holding the paper or fabric in place with your other hand. Knitting needles, skewers, and straws seem to be the favorites, but select something that allows *you* to work comfortably.

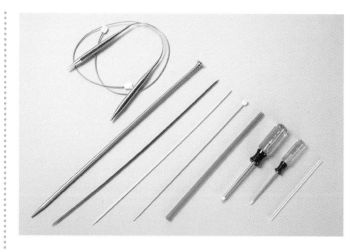

Remember that the size of your form determines the size of the opening in your finished bead. Forms with a smaller diameter create smaller openings in the beads and allow you make a tighter roll. Conversely, a wooden skewer or chopstick may be what you desire for a bead with a wider opening and bulky appearance. If you are a messy glue user, you will want a form that is easy to clean or inexpensive enough to throw away. Plastic and metal forms can be cleaned as necessary, but wood sometimes absorbs enough glue to stick to the bead. As with paper and fabric choices, keep your process in mind when selecting a form. For example, don't use plastic or wood if you will be applying heat to the bead.

When choosing a form, remember that plastic melts and wood burns.

BEAD BINDING
Adhesives

Beads made from paper and fabric need something to hold them together. I prefer adhesives, even though I have yet to learn to keep it off my hands. There are several good choices; again, select the type of adhesive based on the final use of your project as well as the other materials you are using for your beads.

Tacky adhesives are best. They grip the paper or fabric immediately and dry quickly. They come in handy bottles that allow you to clip the top at an angle or straight, making application easier. They clean up nicely. As an added benefit, they do not burn your fingers like hot glue does. Be sure to read the labels on your adhesives. Some require time to set before laundering, some are not laundry safe at any time, some may change the finished appearance of your beads, and some may not be compatible with the fiber you are using.

Some dry adhesives, such as glue sticks, are best for lightweight papers. They are easy to apply and do not bleed through the paper.

Some glues and fabrics simply do not like each other. For example, some dark-colored fabrics will discolor when glue is applied and has dried. Some fabrics will form a hard, shiny surface where the glue has dried.

Finding a glue to use with tulle or organza is not practical unless you plan on having a wrong and right side for these beads. Instead, stitch these beads together or bind them with a fiber wrap. Some adhesives are better suited for paper than for fabric. Some adhesives simply take too long to dry. With thinner papers, like tissue, you may find yourself applying glue to the entire bead because the dyes in the tissue run or change hue when the adhesive is applied. Decoupage products are great for overall coverage. If you'd rather not have a shiny finish, use a glue stick with tissue-weight papers.

Careful selection of your bead and embellishment materials will not only enhance your work, but will also create a lasting impression for admirers.

When you want especially sturdy or rigid beads, apply several coats of clear ultra thick embossing powder (see Embossed Beads on page 28). Initially, these beads will require a tacky glue to hold them together. The adhesive you choose in this case is almost irrelevant because the embossing powders will hold the finished beads together. The Resource section (page 46) lists adhesives and the fibers with which they work best. Don't hesitate to try a new product—you may discover something that works better for you.

Threads

Threads are a magnificent fiber for binding beads. With a few quick stitches and a tiny spot of glue to secure the knot, you will have a bead that can be safely laundered. Thread allows the fabric body to remain soft and pliable; a characteristic that is often lost with glue. Carpet or quilting threads offer more strength than do machine embroidery threads. Two strands of embroidery floss work well, too. You can use creative stitches, such as a French knot, a simple cross-stitch, or a standard straight stitch. Choose a matching or contrasting thread. Tie the threads for extra decoration.

Wire

You can use wire to bind your bead instead of, or in addition to, thread or adhesives. Choose a wire gauge (thickness) appropriate for your bead material and size.

There is no right or wrong choice in adhesives, thread, or wire. You are the bead artist, so the choice is yours. Select the binding for each bead based on aesthetics, function, and durability.

INK, PAINT, AND DYE

If you want to use ink, paint, or dye on your beads, be sure to use appropriate products. If you will be washing a garment with beads on it, be sure to use fabric inks or paints. Read the manufacturer's instructions for information on heat setting, drying time, and suitability for your project. If you use color additives for Heat Shrink Beads (page 30), be certain those additives can tolerate the heat applied during the process. See Resources (page 46) for suggestions. Advance planning is required when using these processes.

Making
BEADS

Throughout this book, there are Additional Design Ideas, which are intended to act as a creative jump-start to get you thinking about ways to expand on the basic techniques. Enjoy the thrill of discovery as you explore, experiment, and have fun!

Chapter 3

Let's make some beads! Assemble all of your materials in a well-lighted workspace. Cover your work surface with old newspaper (new newspaper will transfer into your material) or wax paper if you are using adhesives. Set up a portable, paper-covered work surface if you would like to spend time with family and friends while creating beads. Once you get the hang of it, you will be able to make hundreds of beads in a couple of hours!

Follow these general instructions to make some bead bodies:

Supplies

- Paper or Fabric strips
- Scissors, pinking shears, or a rotary cutter
- Tacky adhesive (e.g., Beacons Fabri-Tac for fabric or Zip-Dry for paper)
- Form (bamboo skewer, straw, or knitting needle)
- Fun fibers: rayon or metallic thread, wool yarn, embroidery floss, silk, thinner yarns, wire

Fabric that is 45″ wide will yield approximately 11 beads. Cutting 1″-wide strips of fabric, you should be able to make approximately 374 beads from 1 yard of fabric.

Standard 8½″ × 11″ paper will yield about 8 beads. Heavier paper will produce twice as many beads, because you'll use a shorter strip for each bead.

Optional Materials

- Tiny brush, cotton swab, or toothpick to apply glue
- Cutting board
- Cutting edge
- Newspaper or plastic to protect your work surface
- Seam sealant (if your fabric unravels easily)
- Pins
- Clothespins (tiny ones from the craft store work well)
- Metal ruler (this is a tremendous help in tearing paper.)
- Craft gloves, such as ProCraft Craft Gloves (see Resources on page 46). I highly recommend these gloves as they are reusable and most every substance is easily washed or peeled off of them!

General Instructions for Making Beads

1. Tear or cut ½″- to 1″-wide strips of fabric or paper. If cutting, use scissors, a rotary cutter, or pinking shears.

2. Cut the strips into 11″ lengths for lightweight paper and 4″ lengths for heavy paper or fabric. Don't worry about being too exact. As the materials change, you will develop a feel for the correct length of material for the type and size of bead you wish to create.

Tear or cut fabric strips approximately 1″ × 4″.

Fabric strips are usually cut on the straight of grain. If you'd like, try a few on a bias (diagonal) cut.

Cut paper results in a finished edge bead. Torn paper creates a softer edge.

If you prefer a finished edge on your fabric beads, cut the fabric strip twice the width that you would like them to finish. Fold or press the unfinished edge toward the center before continuing.

Fabric strips folded for a finished edge

For a frayed edge on the finished end of your fabric bead, fray one short end of the strip. Apply seam sealant if the bead will be subjected to excessive handling (clothes, accessories, etc.). For a decorative edge on the end of a paper bead, use decorative scissors to cut the short end of the strip, or tear against the edge of a ruler for a soft edge.

3. Apply glue to the wrong side of the strip about ⅛″ from one end.

If you have frayed or cut an end of the strip, begin to roll the bead at the opposite end.

Making Beads 15

4. Roll the strip, beginning at the glued end, around your form. Take care to roll tightly in the first round to ensure that the glue holds the first roll to the next.

Rolling a fabric bead

note Be careful not to apply the glue too close to the end of the paper or fabric strip or you will end up gluing the strip to your form.

5. Continue to wrap the body material toward the end of the strip. When you have reached the end of the strip, apply a fine line of adhesive on the wrong side (inside) with your brush, toothpick, or cotton swab to secure the end of the bead.

Gluing the end of a fabric bead

tip

If you are going to wrap your bead with wire or other fiber, you can omit the glue and hold it with a clothespin while you wrap it.

6. The finished bead body should look something like this:

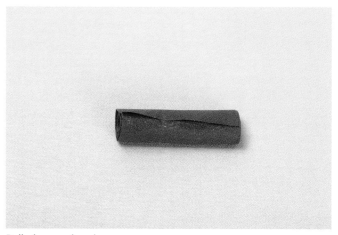

Rolled paper bead

7. Embellish your bead as desired. See Bead Embellishment Techniques (page 19).

CREATING SHAPED BEADS

Now that you have mastered the basic process for making a bead, let's expand beyond the basics. By cutting the fabric or paper strip into a shape other than a rectangle, such as a triangle or a two-pointed "flag," the final body shape of the bead will be different. This can be a great way to showcase a particular section of an interesting piece of fabric or to draw attention to another bead by using the shape to focus interest toward the special bead.

Cone

1. Cut a small rectangle as described in Step 2 of General Instructions for Making Beads (see page 15). Cut the rectangle on the diagonal to make 2 right-angle triangles. Each triangle will be used to make 1 bead.

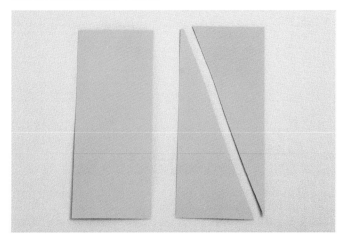

A rectangle cut into 2 triangles.

2. Start rolling from the wide end of the triangle to make the bead. Your final shape will be a cone. This shape is useful if you want to reduce or enlarge an area adjacent to other basic beads or to create a rounded point.

Cone-shaped bead

Ellipse

1. Cut a small rectangle as described in Step 2 of General Instructions for Making Beads (see page 15). Cut an isosceles triangle from the center of the rectangle. This will make an elliptical bead and possibly 2 very small cone-shaped beads from the selvages of the cut.

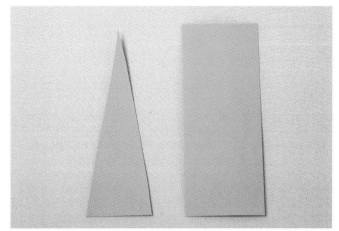

Cut an isosceles triangle.

2. Start rolling from the wide end of the triangle to make the bead. Your final shape will be an ellipse, wider in the center than on the edges.

Elliptical bead

Making your beads in shapes can add an interesting variation to your creative bead making techniques. By using bead bodies made of heavier weight paper or a textile that is slightly rigid (such as Ultrasuede), the shapes of your beads will be more prominent.

Hourglass

1. Cut a small rectangle as described in Step 2 of General Instructions for Making Beads (see page 15). Cut an isosceles triangle from the center. This will make an hourglass bead and possibly 1 tiny elliptical bead.

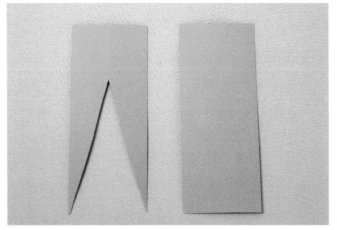

Cutting for an hourglass bead

2. Start at the short straight edge and roll to form the bead. You will need a little extra glue on the 2 "flag" ends of the strip. Your final shape will be an hourglass, wider on the outer edges and narrower in the center.

Hourglass-shaped bead

Use longer strips of material to make the beads fuller. Cutting narrower widths of material will make the beads appear rounder.

Making Multiples of Similar Beads

If you are planning a large project that will require making hundreds of beads, you can make many at one time. By cutting your fabric or paper strips in a wider piece, you can create one long bead. When the adhesive is dry, cut the long bead into smaller units. These beads will have cut edges (straight or pinked) as opposed to frayed edges. Production of these beads is much quicker than one at a time! You can cut them all the same length, or vary the lengths; cut them all at the same angle, or vary the ends.

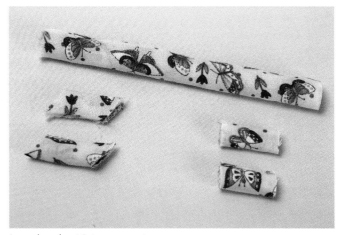

Long bead cut into segments

Additional Design Idea: Create one long bead, and then leave it whole rather than cutting it. You can use this long bead as a feature on an art quilt, to simulate coral on a wall hanging, as a border for a project, or as a frame.

TECHNIQUES

Bead Embellishment Techniques are done after the beads have been rolled. Embellishment techniques are both functional and decorative. Because these embellishments are done after the bead is rolled, they require no advance planning.

Chapter 4

There are so many possibilities for enhancing your beads. To make your planning easier, I've divided the options into two categories, Bead Body Technique and Bead Embellishment Techniques.

Bead Body Techniques	Embellishment Techniques
Fiber Body Beads	Fiber-Tied Beads
Watercolor Beads	Wire-Wrapped Beads
Stamped Beads	Embossed Beads
Double-Layered Beads	Painted Beads
Twisted Beads	Glass Bead Embellishments
Rouched Beads	Heat Shrink Beads
Embroidered Beads	

BEAD BODY TECHNIQUES

Bead Body Techniques are done *before* rolling the beads. Some of the bead body techniques require advance planning for texture and color enhancements before you cut the bead material into strips. Let's explore some of the creative ways to manipulate the fibers before rolling your beads.

Fiber Body Beads

Loose fibers (not spun into "yarn") that can be used for making beads include unspun cotton; washed, carded wool; and flax. You can also use fusible fibers such as Angelina Fibers (see Resources on page 46), to make beads. Consider recycling your leftover sewing or embroidery thread scraps. Or combine many different types of fibers to create interesting textures. Mix colors together or sort fibers into color families before making your beads.

Fiber body beads

Keep a clear sandwich bag near your sewing area to collect thread scraps.

The best technique for making this type of bead is to roll what I call a "blank." This is a basic bead (see General Instructions on page 14) in some neutral color (ivory for light fibers, black or navy for dark fibers). I often use pre-washed 10-ounce cotton canvas; it's a nice strong base for holding the loose fibers together.

1. Following the General Instructions (see page 14), make some paper or fabric beads. Because the blank will be covered with loose fiber, it does not really matter what color fabric or paper you use.

Fabric bead "blanks"

2. Collect some scraps of loose fibers in a pile. You can also cut them in lengths from $\frac{1}{2}''$ to $1''$ (or the length of your blank) if you feel you need a larger pile.

Loose fiber scraps—embroidery floss, skinny yarns, Angelina Fibers

3. Completely cover the blank bead with tacky adhesive such as Fabri-Tac, and then roll it in the loose fibers.

Roll the adhesive covered bead in the loose fibers.

4. Allow at least 10 minutes for drying.

5. Optional: Trim the ends of the loose fiber that extend beyond your bead base.

6. Use another length of fiber or wire to tie the bead to hold the fibers around the bead.

Fiber- and wire-tied beads

Watercolor Beads

Another easy and interesting technique for creative beads is playful coloring. Watercolor paints and paper can give you very artistic results. Although originally created for paper, this technique can also be done on fabric using fabric markers or dyes.

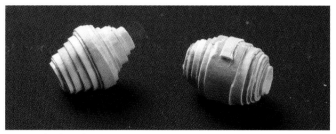
Watercolor beads

1. Use water and a sponge brush to dampen a sheet of lightweight watercolor paper.

2. Choose 2 or 3 colors and spread them across the paper. Vary the lines: straight, curved, thick, and thin.

3. Let the paper dry.

> Use rice paper to make delicate beads.

4. Cut or tear the body material into strips. Choose the length based on the weight of your paper and the desired finished bead size.

Cut your watercolor into strips.

5. Following the General Instructions (see page 14), apply adhesive and roll the beads.

6. Embellish as desired.

> Make plain white beads from watercolor paper. Use the tie-dye technique and wrap a rubber band around the finished bead. Beginning with your lightest watercolor paint, apply one coat. Allow the bead to dry and remove the rubber band. Repeat as many times as you like by repositioning the rubber band. Apply either overall darker colors or spots over the original color.

Stamped Beads

To create a quick, custom paper or fabric before rolling your beads, try rubber-stamping. Keep in mind that you will achieve crisper images on smooth papers and finely woven fabrics. A rough paper or highly textured fabric will result in a more abstract image. Experiment with different stamps on different weights and textures to find the combinations you like best.

Stamped beads

1. Cut a piece of paper or fabric to your desired strip length. You don't have to decide the width yet.

2. Following the ink or paint manufacturer's instructions, apply the ink to your stamp.

3. Stamp your image(s) on the bottom 1″ of your paper or fabric strip.

Stamp on the bottom edge.

4. Heat set your inks, if recommended by the manufacturer.

5. Decide on the finished size of your bead, and cut or tear the stamped material into strips.

tip

Use the edge of a metal ruler to help tearing paper for straight edges.

6. Starting at the unstamped edge, roll your bead with the stamped side facing down. This will allow your stamping to end up on the visible side of the bead.

7. Embellish if desired.

Double-Layered Beads

Combine two layers of paper or fabric when rolling the bead to create both depth and decoration.

Double-layered beads

1. Select 2 strips of material for each bead. Choose a very lightweight material, such as tissue or mulberry paper, or organza, and a slightly sturdier material, such as regular-weight paper or cotton fabric.

2. Tear or cut the material into triangular strips, cutting the lighter-weight material in a narrower strip than the base material so that both will show on the rolled bead.

Cutting for double-layered beads

3. Apply a small amount of adhesive to the wrong side of the bead, and roll the 2 layers as one.

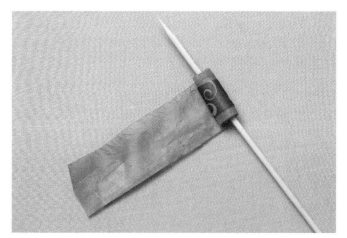

Rolling a double-layered bead

4. Apply a bit more adhesive to secure the ends.

5. Embellish the rolled bead as desired.

Additional Design Ideas: Use metallic paper or fabric for the lighter material.

Twisted Beads

Manipulate the paper or fabric as you finish rolling the bead, to create wonderful beads with a unique finished look.

Twisted beads of paper and fabric

Choose a very flexible paper such as Japanese Washi paper, tissue paper, or nonwoven tissue for the most satisfactory results.

1. Cut the paper or fabric strip approximately ½″ longer than you would for a standard bead.

2. Roll the bead to within 1″ of the end of the material.

3. Hold the rolled bead and form in one hand, place your thumb over the rolled bead. Use your other hand to twist the material once around itself.

Twisting the end of the bead

4. Apply adhesive to secure the end of the material to the bead. The twist that you made will be located at the top of the bead and will appear like a knot, with the closed end under the bead body.

Twisted bead

Further embellish your twisted bead by pulling 6 or 7 strands of fiber (rayon or metallic embroidery threads work well) underneath the knot created by the twist. A spot of adhesive will help keep the fibers secure.

Rouched Beads

Adapted from the ancient Japanese art of making paper beads, this technique is a variation of the twisted bead, using paper-covered floral wire to support the paper and to offer added strength. Use Washi paper to make these beads extra special.

Rouched beads

See Resources (page 46) for sources of Washi paper. Note that the small squares sold for origami are too small for this technique. You will need pieces that are at least 10″ × 14″.

1. Cut a paper strip approximately 2¼″ × 14″.

2. Fold the paper in thirds along the long side.

3. Use a light paper adhesive (a decoupage medium works best) to apply adhesive along the left side. Fold the right side, without adhesive, toward the middle. Apply light pressure with your hand to seal the right side to the left side, creating a paper tube.

Fold and glue the paper strip.

4. Allow to dry.

5. Insert the paper-covered floral wire through the center of the paper tube that you created in Step 3. This very thin gauge will help the bead retain the rouched shape.

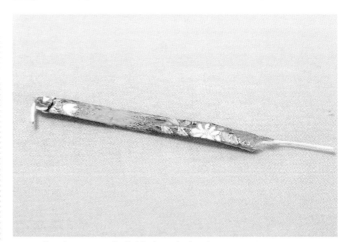

Insert floral wire inside folded and glued paper strip.

6. Fold over the end of the wire and paper (2 folds should be enough) to prevent the wire from slipping out. For added security, crimp the end with pliers.

7. Begin to roll the bead by winding the paper around your form, starting at the end created in Step 6. Overlap the paper slightly to roll the paper around your form about 4 or 5 times to achieve the desired width for your bead.

8. Firmly grasp the wire and scrunch the paper down toward the form. The paper will gather and resemble rouching.

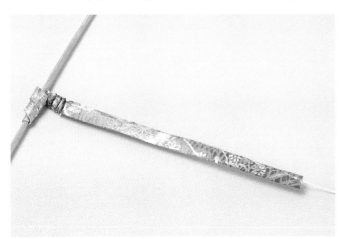

Rolling and scrunching the paper

9. As tightly as you can, without ripping the paper, roll the rouched portion back around the bead, over the previous layer.

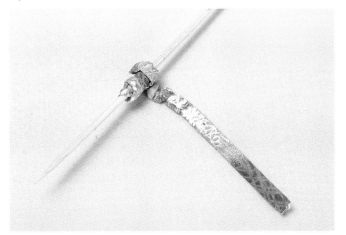

Rolling the rouched bead

10. Continue to scrunch the paper as you roll. The wire will help keep everything in place.

11. Leave about ⅛″ of flat paper at the end. Apply a small drop of quick-drying adhesive to the end, and fold the end back toward the bead.

12. Slip the end under a row of rouching to hide it. The twists that you made should be wound around the entire bead.

tip

You can seal the finished bead with decoupage medium or other sealant. Simply put the bead on a thin wire and dip it in the decoupage medium. Hang to dry. You could also apply sealant gently with a small brush. Allow adequate drying time before you use the bead in a project.

Finished beads

Embroidered Beads

If you are fortunate enough to own (or have a friend who owns) a sewing machine with decorative stitch capabilities or even zigzag stitching, you are going to love this technique! Of course, you can embroider by hand, too.

Embroidered beads

1. Cut strips of fabric in the desired strip length, 2½ times the width of the desired finished bead. This will enable you to create a bead with a neat, finished edge that highlights the stitching! If you are using felt for your embroidered beads, you'll only need a single layer of fabric.

> If you want to make multiple embroidered beads, cut and embroider a longer strip, then cut the long embroidered strip into several lengths for your beads. Add some seam sealant on the ends of the beads to prevent unraveling.

2. Fold the edges in toward the center to the desired finished width. Pin at the top, or use basting spray, instead of pinning, to keep the folds in place.

3. Use a complementary thread color, embroider down the center of your folded fabric strip. Add a piece of tear-away stabilizer if you are using a flimsy fabric or if you prefer a more stable base for embroidery.

Embroider the center of the fabric strip.

> You can embroider the last one-inch along the side edge of the bead instead of the end for a slightly different look.

4. If you used a stabilizer, remove it now.

> You can leave the stabilizer in if you want additional body strength.

5. Roll the bead with the right side facing down. This will allow your embroidery to end up on the outside of the bead.

6. Embellish as desired, but don't hide your embroidery stitches!

> Embroider the edges of the fabric strip to finish them. Use a blanket stitch or a shaped satin stitch, or serge them with variegated thread!

BEAD EMBELLISHMENT TECHNIQUES

These techniques give you an opportunity to further enhance your beads by using embellishments.

Many of these techniques are most easily accomplished if the bead is still on the form. The stable form helps the bead maintain its shape while you tie, bind, or otherwise manipulate the bead.

Fiber-Tied Beads

This is probably the easiest and quickest embellishment. Start with a simple bead, choose a complementary fiber, and wrap up some fun, creative beads!

Fiber-tied beads

Supplies

- 1 blank bead
- Eyelash yarn or other fibers
- Form (knitting needle, skewer, or whatever you used when rolling the bead)

Step-by-Step

1. Using a dry bead is important. Adhesives sometimes soak through the paper or fabric. If the bead is still tacky, the adhesive will get on the fibers. Once the fibers get sticky, they are difficult to use and do not produce the best results. When the bead is ready, take the dry bead, and place it on the form you used to roll it.

2. Wrap 1 or more fibers around the bead.

3. Secure with a square knot and a drop of adhesive or seam sealant.

4. Trim the ends.

For even more interest, use another fiber and tie again, or tie one time using multiple fibers.

Wire-Wrapped Beads

Another simple and secure way to embellish your beads is to tie them with metal or plastic-coated wire. Twist the ends in loops or spirals, add glass beads, wrap the wire, or combine sizes and colors of wire for extra interest.

Wire-wrapped beads in paper and fabric

Supplies

- Blank bead
- 7″ length of wire (24- or 26-gauge wire is easiest to use.)
- Round-nosed pliers

note Wire wrapping is not recommended for beads that will be on clothing.

Step-by-Step

1. Place the bead on the form for support.

2. Wrap the wire twice around the bead.

3. Twist the wire around itself 2 or 3 times.

4. Use round-nosed pliers to form the wire ends into spirals. Flatten as necessary.

tip

Make spirals on the ends of the wire in triangle, square, or round shapes. Use round- or flat-nosed pliers to help you achieve a tighter edge.

Embossed Beads

Embossing the paper or fabric after rolling your bead adds great visual interest, texture, and strength.

Embossed beads

1. Cut a piece of paper, fabric, or Tyvek for your bead.

2. Select a form that can withstand heat, and have a potholder nearby.

3. Roll the strip into the desired bead shape.

4. Pour ultra-thick embossing powder into a container that will allow you to submerge the entire bead.

tip

A clear plastic sandwich bag is great to use when embossing beads. If the bag is resealable, leave the embossing powder in the bag so it will be ready for the next time.

5. Following the manufacturer's instructions for the embossing ink you are using, cover the entire bead with ink by rolling it on the pad or applying generously with a sponge-tip applicator.

tip

For best coverage, use Ultra Thick Embossing Enamel (UTEE) from Ranger Ink (see Resources on page 46). Regular powders will create a nice decorative touch, but will not strengthen the bead or allow you to cover it entirely.

6. With the freshly inked bead still on the form, roll it in embossing powder until it's completely covered. Remove the excess UTEE from the end of the form.

tip

If you own a melting pot, omit steps 4-7 and heat the UTEE in your melting pot. Dip the beads into the pot to coat them with UTEE.

7. Preheat your heat gun, and hold the bead over a protected surface. Melt the embossing powder.

UTEE will take longer than regular embossing powders to heat up, so be patient as you turn the form and melt the enamel.

Turn the form as you heat the embossing powder to ensure that the coating is smooth and even.

8. Allow the bead to cool. Examine it for imperfections and apply additional coats of ink and embossing powder as needed. The first coat may be bumpy but it should even out with additional applications of embossing powder.

Try adding lighter or colored powders to the embossing powder for interesting effects. If you purchase your embossing powder in a clear color, you can create custom finishes by adding very small amounts of other embossing powders or by adding Pearl EX Pigments.

9. Embellish if desired.

To add additional texture, stamp the bead while the embossing powder is still warm. Or, while the bead is still warm, mix colored, lightweight embossing powders together on the bead after the initial powder has been applied. Reheat (twirl the bead slowly during heating for a marbled effect). Or wrap wire (not plastic coated) around the bead prior to applying embossing powder. Emboss and remove the wire, to add a texture to the bead.

Painted Beads

Painting the beads after forming can be a great way to highlight them. Use metallic paints to make the fiber art beads catch the light!

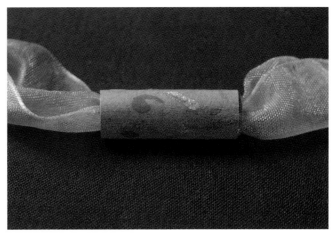

Painted paper beads

1. Place the bead on a protected surface.

2. Use a small paintbrush, paint marker, or toothpick to doodle spots, stripes, or dots on the bead.

Painting the ends of fabric beads not only adds color but also prevents frayed edges.

3. Allow adequate drying time.

4. Embellish further with fibers to coordinate with paint color.

Glass Bead Embellishments

Glass beads can be added to either the fiber wrap or the wire wrap, or as a stand-alone technique. Glass beads provide not only extra color but also some additional sheen to your beads.

Glass bead embellishments

1. String glass beads onto a piece of embroidery floss, beading thread, or thin jewelry wire.

Use a beading needle if you have trouble stringing your beads onto the fiber.

2. Wrap thread or wire around the bead twice. Twist the wire once, or tie a knot in the thread.

3. Twist the strung beads in place around the bead in a band of color.

4. Tie a knot or twist the wire on the backside of the beaded string.

5. Add a touch of jewelry adhesive such as Gem-Tac (see Resources on page 46) to secure the knot.

You can sew or glue glass seed beads in small clusters on top of a fiber-tied beads. Or try using Liquid Beadz to apply the glass beads with a palette knife or disposable plastic knife for overall coverage.

Heat Shrink Beads

This technique involves altering the bead material with heat, also known as heat distress. Many of these synthetic materials are difficult to glue. When heated, they may shrink or distort, virtually melting to adhere themselves to the fibers surrounding them making adhesive unnecessary.

Heat shrink beads

Always perform heat shrink techniques outside or in a well-ventilated room, or wear a protective mask to prevent breathing fumes that might be generated.

note   Be careful of your work surface and surrounding materials.

Experimentation is key to successful, creative, heat shrunk beads. Many natural fibers, including wool felt, are resistant to heat. Other fibers, such as chiffon, organza, interfacing, and Ultrasuede, offer interesting, yet very different, textural results when heated. Be aware that each model of heat gun performs differently. Try several different materials to see what works best for you.

note   No matter which combination you are experimenting with, remember to use a metal form and a potholder to protect yourself.

Making Heat Shrink Beads From Organza, Chiffon, or Synthetic Felt

1. Cut or tear the fabric into the strip width you want for your bead. It will shrink slightly, so if you require an exact finished size, experiment with a few different widths to see which results in the desired finished size. As a rule of thumb, shrinkage in the width is roughly 10%.

2. Roll the bead. Instead of adhesive, use a metal pin with a metal head to secure the fabric when the bead has been rolled.

3. Preheat your heat gun. Proceed slowly to achieve the look you want. From about 4″ to 6″ away from the bead, apply heat, protecting your hands from the heat. The fabric will melt, scorch, or completely disintegrate if the heat is applied for too long or if the heat source is held too close to the bead.

You may wish to embellish the piece of fabric prior to rolling the bead by sewing decorative stitching on the strips of fabric. If you use cotton thread in both the needle and bobbin, the stitching will remain intact after the fabric has melted or shrunk. The stitching will create interesting surface designs. Metallic threads often remain intact as well. Most polyester and rayon threads distort when heat is applied. Experiment with your thread and your heat gun to see what works best for you.

Making Heat Shrink Beads From Tyvek

When using Tyvek as your bead material, softening it first makes it easier to roll. Crumple the material in your hand several times and then submerge it in water. Allow it to air dry before proceeding. This is a fast-drying material. *Do not put the material in the dryer* because Tyvek is heat-sensitive.

1. With a brush, splatter paint, or spray bottle apply concentrated liquid dye, ink, or acrylic paints to the material before cutting it into strips. You do not need to be artistic or even neat, just use a lot of color. You can also apply ink to the Tyvek after you form the bead, just cover it in embossing poder (see page 28 for more information).

Appling color to Tyvek

2. Give the Tyvek an aged appearance after painting or dying by sanding it with a fine sandpaper to remove some of the color. Or crumple it and then lightly apply a metallic paint to highlight the wrinkles.

3. Cut strips 8″ × the width you wish your bead to be.

4. Roll the beads.

5. Bind the bead using very light-gauge wire, such as beading wire or metallic thread, or hold it together with a clothespin.

6. Preheat your heat gun. Starting at one end, lightly pass the heat gun over the bead. Do not linger at a single spot too long, or the materials will self-destruct.

7. Do not handle the bead immediately after using the heat gun. The polymers have melted, and they are very hot. Allow at least 30 seconds to cool.

Fold and pin the Tyvek into interesting shapes, such as a triangle or square. With heat shrinking, you can accomplish many shapes that are not achievable with the regular rolling technique.

Creating
With Beads

Now it is time to use those beads that you've had so much fun making. Your creative mind has probably been churning with great ideas already; if not, here are some ideas to give you inspiration.

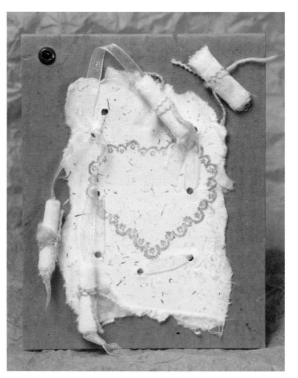

Chapter 5

NOTE CARDS

Special note cards don't need to take forever to make. Start with purchased card stock, add stamped images, cut or torn paper and fabric, found objects, ribbon, or wire. Sew or glue your fiber art beads as the finishing touch. You'll never want to run to the store for a last-minute card again!

Note cards embellished with creative beads

tip

Here's a great rainy day project for creating a stockpile of beads and note cards for future use. Have your children make beads using the Sunday comics or old magazines. They can glue the beads into a pattern or design on a card for an upcoming birthday party or for a special card for their grandparents.

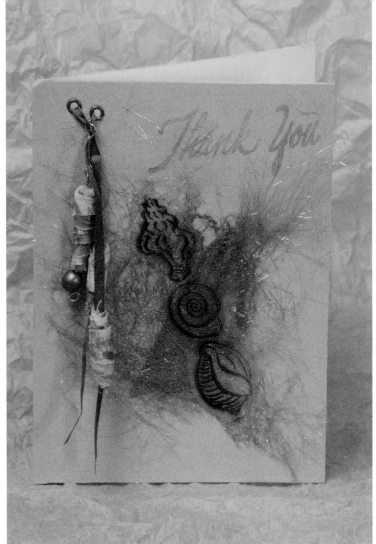

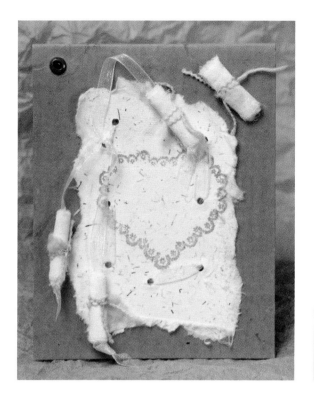

GIFT BAGS

Make the presentation of your gift as memorable as the gift itself by embellishing plain purchased bags with your original beads! If you are really lucky, a good friend or family member might recycle the bag back to you on your next special day!

Embellished gift bags

tip

As an extra touch, decorate a wooden clothespin with paper scraps and a special bead. Use the clip to hold the gift card on the bag or to keep the bag's contents safe from peeping eyes!

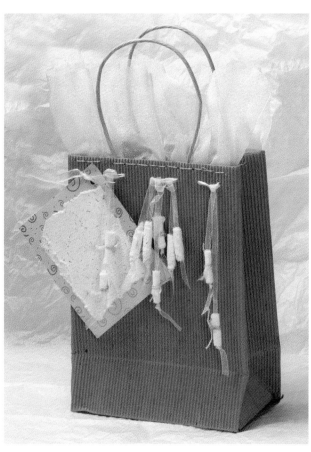

PAPER COLLAGE

Paper collage can be so satisfying. Start with a large sheet of paper. Layer fragments of other paper, both torn and cut. Add a few found objects and your fabulous fiber art beads to create a special wallhanging for yourself or to give as a special gift.

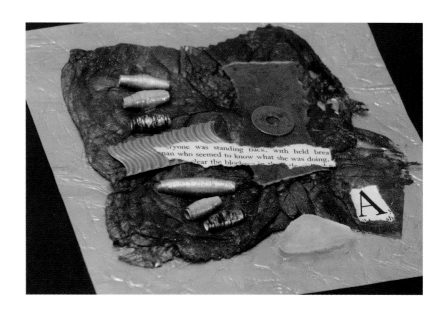

tip

Create a series of collages, relating them by color or by theme and display them together in your home as an artistic, stylish statement.

CUSTOM JOURNAL

A custom journal might be the perfect gift for a friend. Make one to use as your special place to jot down creative ideas. Purchase a hardbound blank book, then add a fabric collage, fibers, and creative beads.

PAPIER-MÂCHÉ BOX

The next time you need a special gift box, embellish a papier-mâché box from the craft store. It's easier than it looks. Cover the box with colored tissue paper and embellish the lid with ribbon-tied beads. You can be sure the recipient will continue to use the box to keep treasures safely inside.

SCARF OR WRAP

Start with a luscious chiffon or organza fabric, and sew decorative stitches, then add your extra-special embroidered beads and a scrumptious fringe. You'll be ready for any special occasion!

tip

If you like to knit, try adding some of your creative beads onto a scarf near both ends. Add more beads to the fringe. Want an even quicker project to give as a gift? Buy a knitted scarf and add your unique beads to the fringe.

Use your favorite bag pattern or simply cut a rectangle. The bags shown here all started with a 14″ x 22″ rectangle from each of two fabrics: one for the lining and one or more joined for the outside of the bag. Cut a third rectangle of interfacing if you like.

Handbags featuring creative beads

This pink evening bag was folded into thirds to create the flap.

tip

If you paint and stamp Tyvek for your bag, spray it with a multipurpose sealant when your design is complete.

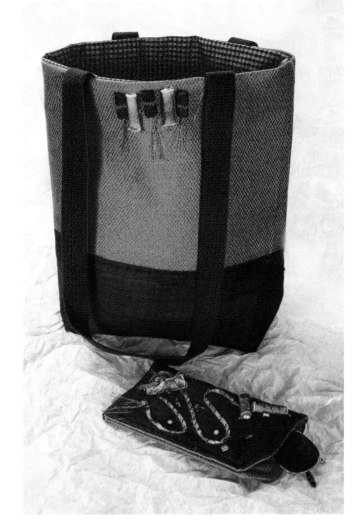

Sew or glue beads to the fringe that you added. String beads onto fibers, then glue or sew these to the outside of your purse.

Handles: Make handles from fabric strips, purchase wood handles, or sew cotton webbing to serve as handles on your original bag. Add fringe, dangle beads, stamp, and paint on Tyvek for a fun bag. Dress up a favorite outfit by making a coordinating tote for your next shopping excursion!

HANDBAG EMBELLISHMENTS

Create multi-fiber fringe for your bag by looping several different fibers down as far as you want the fringe to dangle, then loop them back toward the top. Sew or pin the fringe in place at the top edge of the bag as you fold it. Cut the fringe or leave it looped. Sew approximately ½″ from the top edge of the bag to keep the fringe in place.

An easy way to get the beads onto the fringe is to make a faux needle. Fold a wire in half and place the bead over the wire. Thread a piece of fringe through the folded end of the wire. Pull the bead onto the fringe and remove the wire.

JEWELRY

For maximum impact and interest, combine your creative beads with purchased glass beads, metal parts from the hardware store, or buttons from your button collection. A quick trip to the bead or craft store for wire and small tools, and you're ready to create custom jewelry.

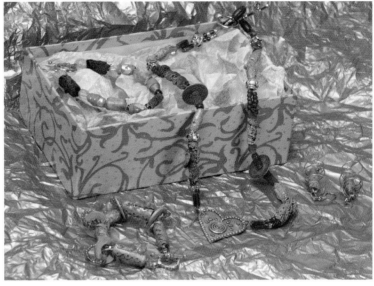

Creative bead jewelry

Making Jewelry From Creative Beads

1. Experiment with different combinations of beads, arranging them on a flat surface.

2. Place the clasp at the ends. Measure again to be sure the bracelet or necklace is the desired length.

3. Step back and look at your design. Check for symmetry and a pleasing color arrangement. Rearrange as you like.

4. Cut the wire 3″ longer than the desired finished length of your piece.

5. Following the manufacturer's instructions, string a crimping bead onto the wire. Add the clasp. Bend the wire about 1″ from the end and feed it back through the crimping bead. Crimp the bead with your pliers to secure the end of the wire and to hold the clasp in place.

6. String your beads and repeat the crimping at the other end before adding the other half of the clasp.

tip

A standard bracelet is about 7″ long. Use this measurement as a guideline, and adjust as necessary add extra for more dangle.

LAMPSHADE

Creative beads and some ribbon make the perfect embellishment for purchased lampshades.

Art quilts are a wonderful way to express yourself or to test new ideas. You can combine several techniques, similar to the project shown here, or simply use a variation of one technique again and again. The sky is the limit with this project as inspiration. When you are finished with your original wall art, attach fiber loops to the back to hang your piece, and get ready for the admiration that will come your way!

Sign makers use Tyvek all the time. You can cut it to standard paper size and feed it through your printer. Think about using digital images, text, and copies of scanned photographs for your art quilts.

One World nine-patch quilt includes fabric, paper, Tyvek, beads, and more.

 tip

When using a machine to sew paper, select a medium stitch length to prevent tearing or perforating the paper. If the stitches are too close together, the paper will just fall away from the stitching.

CONCLUDING YOUR CREATIVE BEAD ADVENTURE

I hope you enjoyed working with the techniques in *Creative Beads from Paper and Fabric*. I also hope you were able to stretch yourself and your techniques and that you have learned something new.

The greatest component of creativity is that it ties us together. When we share artistic techniques formally through a book, or informally over a cup of coffee, we give a small piece of ourselves away. One creator's idea is tried, shared, improved, and varied in so many ways that it is no longer just one person's idea—it becomes an integral part of us all. Whether it is through song, painting, sewing, quilting, gardening, lab experiments, or house painting, by sharing your ideas, *you better the world.*

RESOURCES

A note about the Resources: These products worked for me. Not every artist experiences the same results. Something as simple as the weather can affect product performance. I highly recommend that you test small samples and follow the manufacturers' instructions, especially when working with adhesives.

Each product is referenced by the name on the label.

Adhesives

Product	Use
Aleene's Okay to Wash It! (www.duncancrafts.com/crafts)	Fabrics to be washed
Aleene's Twice as Tacky (www.duncancrafts.com/crafts	Textured papers
Fabri-Tac (www.beaconcreates.com)	All fabric
Gem-Tac (www.beaconcreates.com)	Heavy embellishments
Paper-Tac (www.beaconcreates.com	Archival papers
Zip Dry (www.beaconcreates.com)	Most papers

Fabrics

Hancock Fabrics (www.hancockfabrics.com)

JoAnn Fabrics (www.joann.com)

MeinkeToy (www.meinketoy.com)

Fibers

Adornments by EK Success (www.eksuccess.com)

Angelina Fibers (www.meadowbrookglitter.com/angelina/splash.html)

Bernat's Boa (www.bernat.com)

Colorlash (www.plymouthyarn.com)

DMC Embroidery Thread (www.dmc-usa.com)

Lion Brand's Fun Fur (www.lionbrand.com)

Forms

14″ metal knitting needle; sizes 3, 5, 8, 11 (www.coatsandclark.com)

Bamboo skewers, available at grocery or party stores

Ink and Embossing Powders

Brilliance Ink (www.tsukineko.com)

Crystal Dye-Based Ink Pad (www.deltacrafts.com)

Encore! Ultimate Metallic Stamp Pad (www.tsukineko.com)

Ultra Thick Embossing Enamel (www.rangerink.com)

VersaCraft (formerly Fabrico) (www.tsukineko.com)

Miscellaneous Products

Craft Gloves: I highly recommend these gloves as they are reusable and most every substance is easily washed or peeled off of them. Posh Impressions (www.poshimpressions.com)

FabricMate Dual Shader markers (www.yasutomo.com)

Fray Check liquid seam sealant (www.dritz.com)

Liquid Beadz self-adhesive beads (www.decoart.com)

Paper making kits and supplies (www.arnoldgrummer.com)

Paint Markers (www.krylon.com)

Rotary cutter and pad (www.olfa.com)

Tulip Ultra Soft Brushable Fabric Paint (www.duncancrafts.com/crafts)

Tyvek, purchase new material as yard goods from Meinke Toy (www.meinketoy.com), or recycle used mailing envelopes.

Papers

Handmade paper (www.hobbylobby.com)

Handmade paper pad (www.provocraft.com)

Indian handmade paper (www.papersbycatherine.com)

Nonwoven tissue from If It's Paper! (www.xpedx.com)

Washi paper, Japanese paper and origami supplies (www.origami.com.au)—Yes, they are in Australia, but visit the sight because the choices and prices are very good. If you have a small retail paper supply store nearby, they may be able to purchase the 10″× 14″ sheets (also known as B4) for you from Aitoch, Inc. (www.aitoch.com).

Scissors

Cutter Bee Scissors (www.eksuccess.com)

Decorative paper scissors (www.fiskars.com)

Threads

Robison-Anton (www.robison-anton.com)

Sulky (www.sulky.com)

Wire

Fun Wire (www.tonerplastics.com)

WireForm (www.amaco.com)

Other Retail Sources

A.C. Moore (www.acmoore.com)

Hobby Lobby (www.hobbylobby.com)

Michaels (www.micheals.com)

The Enchanted Cottage, Lewisville, NC (www.enchantedcottagenc.com)

ABOUT THE AUTHOR

Professional craft designer Ann Krier specializes in original, ecclectic designs using fiber art techniques. A seamstress since age 10, she has always enjoyed all forms of art and craft. Her current interests lie in finding new and exciting ways to incorporate not-so-traditional materials, such as loose mill fibers, Tyvek, paper, sheet metal, foils, and recycled materials, into her project designs. As a material-based designer and owner of Design One World Inc., it is her goal to produce fun and unique ideas to share with her students and readers. She believes that understanding the materials helps each artist develop to his or her full creative potential.

Originally from upstate New York, Ann has been an executive, a kitchen designer, a manufacturer's representative, and a certified food service professional in the commerical appliance industry. She regulary applies her business experience in sales and marketing, and associated material practice to her designs. Ann belongs to the American Sewing Guild, Associated Artists, Craft & Hobby Association , and the Society of Craft Designers. She is a graduate of Muskingum College and a veteran of more than 200 hours of hands-on creative workshops.

Ann lives in the Piedmont Triad Region of North Carolina with her husband, Jim and busy family. She is the mother of four "children" Mike, Brett, Maggie Sue, and "Murphy". In addition to creative endeavors, Ann enjoys skiing, camping, biking, and kayaking and marvels at the music of Jimmy Buffett.

Most warm, sunny days, you will find her in the pool, playing games with the other children. Other days, you will find her "glued" to one of her design projects and the computer, surrounded by a pile of "art stuff".

"... fabric, paper, scissors and glue …

A perfect day !"